IMAGES OF ENGLAND

WAVERTREE

IMAGES OF ENGLAND

WAVERTREE

MIKE CHITTY AND DAVID FARMER

TEMPUS

Frontispiece: This photograph of Sandown Lane in the 1890s was found among a collection of glass lantern slides, the majority of which were anonymous family and wedding portraits. The pictures were taken by Edward Newton Ellis, a photographer whose father ran a fishmonger and fruiterer's shop at No.2 High Street, Wavertree. The family lived above the shop – and this was the view from one of their windows.

First published 2004

Tempus Publishing Limited
The Mill, Brimscombe Port,
Stroud, Gloucestershire, GL5 2QG
www.tempus-publishing.com

© Mike Chitty and David Farmer, 2004

The right of Mike Chitty and David Farmer to be identified as the Authors
of this work has been asserted in accordance with the
Copyrights, Designs and Patents Act 1988.

British Library Cataloguing in Publication Data.
A catalogue record for this book is available from the British Library.

ISBN 0 7524 3068 8

Typesetting and origination by Tempus Publishing Limited.
Printed in Great Britain.

Contents

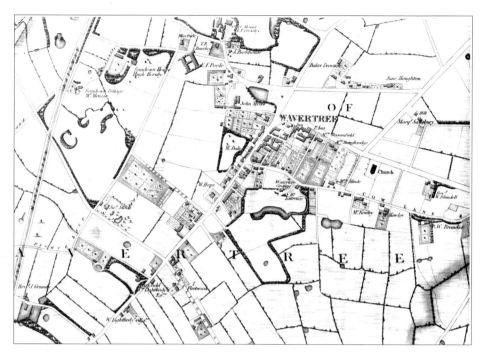

Jonathan Bennison's *Map of the Town and Port of Liverpool with their Environs... from actual survey* gives us a good idea of what Wavertree was like in 1835. It shows the village concentrated between Sandown Lane and Church Road, and names some of the property owners in the surrounding area. Hugh Hornby is at Sandown Hall, John Myers at Lake House, Henry Lawrence at Wavertree Grange, James Stock at Westdale and Thomas Fleetwood at the Rose Brewery.

Acknowledgements

Almost half of the photographs in this volume come from David Farmer's personal collection of postcards. The scenes of Wavertree in 1978-82 are derived from Mike Chitty's colour slides. The remainder of the pictures have been contributed, directly or indirectly, by a variety of individuals, including Primrose Agbamu, Sheilagh Birch, Ed Bodington, Richard Bottrill, Dr Rodney Brandon, the late Winifred Carlin, Christina Clarke, Fred Clarke, Len Dukes, Len Dyke, Joyce Edwards, Janet England, Vin Foster, Florence Gersten, Gary Griffith, the late Palma Hayes, Lucille Henry, Dave Hobster, Margaret Kavanagh, Jim Larkin, Janet Little, Eileen Lowe, the late Mabel Lowe, Sylvia McMillan, the late John Maw, Eileen May, the late Ken May, Stella Moore, Pamela Norrington, Marjorie Osborn, Reg Plunkett, David Power, Colin Pyle, Bob Seddon, Susan Smith and Betty Ward. The cover picture is reproduced with the permission of the Liverpool Libraries and Information Services. The authors' thanks also go to Eddie Cameron, Pam Harvey, Ian Henry, Stan Neill, Joan Williams and others who have supplied background information, to the members and Committee of the Wavertree Society for their encouragement – and to anyone who has inadvertently been omitted from the above list.

Introduction

Wavertree is a suburb of Liverpool, situated between two and four miles east of the city centre. In the nineteenth century it was a separate township, with its own Local Board and its own town hall. Before that, it was a sleepy agricultural village within the Hundred of West Derby.

Unlike Liverpool, Wavertree was mentioned in the Domesday Book! It was then described as *Wauretreu,* and later variants included Wavertre and Wartre. There have been several theories as to the origin of the name, the most plausible being 'the place by the common pond'. It would certainly appear that the existence of a local source of water – the spring which fed the Monks' Well and Wavertree Lake – was the reason why a settlement first developed here. The underlying sandstone, rising to form hills to the north and south-east of the village, also meant that the land was relatively dry and suitable for building.

Although Bronze Age burial urns were found in Victoria Park in 1867, and the Monks' Well in Mill Lane bears the date 1414, there is very little visible evidence remaining of early Wavertree. Nor was there 90-100 years ago, when the majority of the postcard photographs in this book were taken. 'Old' Wavertree then consisted of the few farm cottages, the windmill and other relics which survived from before the nineteenth century, and the Georgian mansions which had been built by Liverpool merchants around the edge of the original village. For during the course of the Victorian and Edwardian eras, the character of Wavertree – as of many other areas within easy reach of the growing town and port of Liverpool – had been dramatically transformed.

The early, wealthy 'immigrants' required local services, and new rows of small houses were therefore built to accommodate people such as gardeners, laundresses and coachmen. The village High Street changed from being a cluster of cottages to a street of shops and other business premises. As Liverpool grew, so Wavertree also became a popular place to visit – not least for a drink in one of the pubs like the Lamb or the Coffee House. Then, during the nineteenth century, it became feasible for the middle classes, rather than just the wealthy, to live in Wavertree and commute daily into town to work. The establishment of the Wavertree Local Board of Health in 1851 meant that there was now an elected body with responsibility for matters such as sewerage, paving and street lighting, all of which increased the attractiveness of the township as a place to live and for landowners to develop.

The township of Wavertree covered quite an extensive area. The boundary followed, in part, such present-day roads as Binns Road, Queens Drive, Childwall Priory Road, Gipsy Lane, Druids Cross Road, Green Lane, Rose Lane, Penny Lane, Smithdown Road, Webster Road and Spofforth Road. It seems possible that the southern 'spur' of the township, which included the slopes of Mossley Hill, had once been part of *Esmedune* (commemorated today by the name Smithdown Road) which was recorded in the Domesday Book but the location of which has provoked debate among scholars. Whether or not this was the case, few people would today regard Mossley Hill as part of Wavertree. So, for the purpose of this book, Wavertree has been defined as the 'L15' (Liverpool 15) postal district.

Between 1851 and 1921 the population of the township increased more than tenfold, from 4,000 to 46,000. By the outbreak of war in 1914, virtually the whole of the western part – in other words the area between the village and the one-time Liverpool boundary – had become covered in a mass of streets and houses, interspersed with the occasional church or industrial building. There were large railway yards, and the main roads were lined with shops.

In fact, Liverpool had outgrown its official boundaries to such an extent that, in 1895, the city was expanded to take in the previously independent townships of Wavertree, West Derby and Walton-on-the-Hill. Liverpool Corporation then embarked on a programme of public service provision in its newly acquired areas, including libraries, swimming pools, electric tramways and new roads – such as Queens Drive, running along the eastern edge of the old Wavertree township – all of which increased the pressure for development still further.

In 1910 Wavertree Nook – the north-eastern corner of the township – became the site of an experiment in housing reform and town planning when Liverpool Garden Suburb Tenants Ltd began building an estate of houses for rent, complete with the gardens and recreational facilities which had generally been lacking in the so-called 'bye-law' housing areas built during the previous forty years. This new low-density style set the pattern for the further wave of housing development, both by the city council for rent and by private builders for sale to owner-occupiers, which took place in the 1920s and 1930s.

Today the old village of Wavertree, and the houses, streets and public open spaces which have been created around it during the past two centuries, are firmly embedded within the much larger built-up area of 'Greater Liverpool', which now extends to about eight miles from the city centre. But the area still retains much of its original character, and two districts – Wavertree Village and the Garden Suburb – are now designated as Conservation Areas. The object of this book is to illustrate the changes which have taken place, to record some past events in the life of the community, and to bring together some notes on the history of the area which, it is hoped, will be of interest to past, present and future residents.

Mike Chitty
Local History Secretary
The Wavertree Society

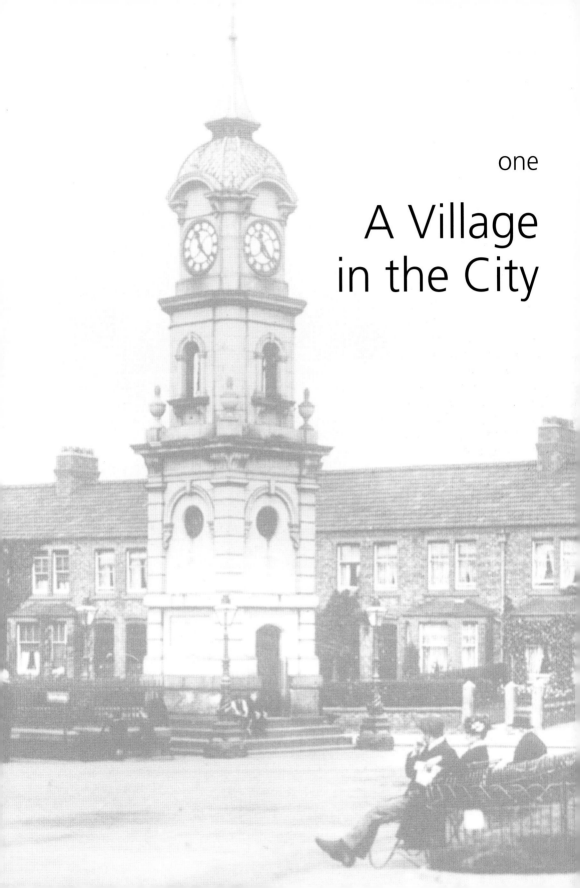

one

A Village
in the City

*W*hat is now the High Street, Liverpool 15, was traditionally called just 'Wavertree Village'. Over the past 200 years it has been transformed from a lane at the heart of an agricultural village to a busy suburban thoroughfare. Reminders of the past include Wavertree Town Hall, the Picton Clock Tower and the one-time Smallest House in England.

This was the view from the roof of the Abbey Cinema in 1979. The former tram shelter in the foreground had long since lost its original purpose, though the public toilets on either side were still in use. The Picton Clock Tower presided over Wavertree Village, as it had done for almost 100 years and as it still does today. The BP petrol station on the corner of Church Road North and the High Street catered for motorists heading from Childwall to the city centre.

Right: The Picton Clock Tower was erected in 1884 by James Picton, in memory of his wife Sarah Pooley who had died in 1879 after fifty years of happy marriage. Picton lived locally, at Sandyknowe in Mill Lane, and was an architect as well as being chairman of the Wavertree Local Board of Health. This postcard view dates from the early years of the twentieth century. It shows the short terrace of gabled houses built in 1899 just off Childwall Road. To the right of the clock tower is the underground public urinal – 'the hole in the ground' as it was known locally – the construction of which was the very last act of the short-lived Wavertree Urban District Council in 1895!

Below: A view from the High Street in the early 1920s. This is in some ways a 'puzzle picture' as the building immediately behind the clock tower has not been found on any map. It is believed to have been a pavilion serving the White Star Line's sports ground, between Church Road North and Lance Lane. The building had a short life, as local residents successfully claimed that it was illegal to erect any structure on this land called 'Wavertree Green'. It was only in 1938 that the ruling was overturned and the Abbey Cinema was built on the site.

The Picton Clock Tower from Church Road North, *c.* 1912. In the background is the Lamb Inn –
before the stone porch was built – and the row of houses (originally Greenside Terrace) at the top
end of the High Street. The people on the seat were perhaps waiting for a tram.

This earlier postcard view shows the corner of Church Road North and the High Street, before the
eruption of advertising hoardings which later characterised the junction. The cast-iron 'dolphin'
lamps at the base of the clock tower then supported globe-shaped gas lanterns. The Clock Tower
pub, beyond, offers Jones's Knotty Ash Ale.

The motor age had arrived in Wavertree, with a taxi office alongside Walker's Lamb Hotel. The taxis were operated by Charles James, who later gave his name to the 'Home James' coach company.

At 105 High Street, just below the Lamb, was Stephen Chesters' butchers shop.

Left: The caption of this Edwardian postcard reads 'Smallest House in England, Wavertree, Liverpool'. The address of the house was 95 High Street, and it measured just 6ft wide by 14ft deep. On the left of the picture is the Cock & Bottle pub, and on the right is Mrs Fanny Parr's tobacconists shop.

Below left: The Smallest House, *c.* 1904. The house was only built around 1850, in what had been a passageway between two older buildings. There are many stories of the people – including some remarkably large families! – who once lived there.

Below right: The last inhabitants of the Smallest House, Mr & Mrs Richard Greaves, moved out in 1925. It remained empty until about 1952, when one of the side walls was knocked through and it became part of the Cock & Bottle. This photograph was taken in 1969, by which time No.97 had become McLinden's refrigerator showroom. In 1998 the owners of the Cock & Bottle restored the external appearance of the house, though it remains an integral part of the pub.

The occupiers of No.95 High Street were conscious of living in one of the 'sights' of Wavertree. A magnifying glass applied to the original postcard – which is dated 1906 – reveals the words 'Smallest House in England' on a notice in the ground-floor window.

Wavertree Town Hall, at 89 High Street, was built in 1872 as the headquarters of the Wavertree Local Board of Health. This postcard was issued in the 1920s, by which time the effects of smoke pollution had become all too apparent.

This photograph of the town hall dates from about 1905. The township of Wavertree had been absorbed by the city of Liverpool ten years earlier. Etched into the ground-floor windows are the words 'Liverpool Corporation District Office', but over the front door is displayed the emblem of the former township: a tree surrounded by the words *Sub Umbra Floresco*. 'I flourish in the shade' is perhaps a reference to Wavertree's proud independence from big-brother Liverpool down the road. The town hall was designed by local architect John Elliot Reeve, who lived in Sandown Lane. Behind the offices was a large ballroom which was available for hire.

Wavertree High Street was home to a variety of family businesses, some of which remained until relatively recent years. Among them – seen in this photograph of 1978 – were Wattersons the chemist and Hicks the baker. This block of shops and commercial premises dates from the 1860s, shortly before the town hall was built, but the house on the right (No.85 High Street) is a reminder of the original domestic scale of the village.

John Hicks' employees pose for the camera, outside his bakery and warehouse at 83 High Street, in the early twentieth century. The posters for Lactifer (food for calves), Thorley's (for horses) and Ovum (for chickens) demonstrate that Wavertree was not yet entirely urbanised.

A Hicks bread van delivering in North Drive, Victoria Park.

This postcard view of Chesnut Grove dates from the early 1900s, before the houses numbered 11-21 were built. On the far right of the picture is the terrace of houses in Laburnum Grove, beyond the Catholic church and Presbytery. Was the little girl intending to sweep the whole street, or was she just posing for the cameraman?

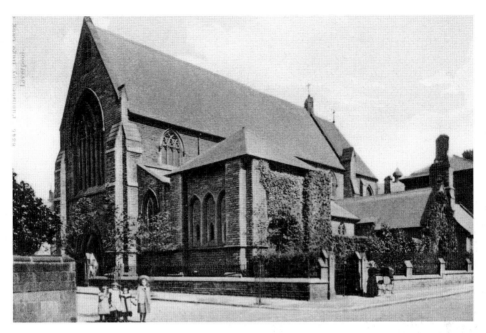

Between 1885-1887 the Church of Our Lady of Good Help was built in Chesnut Grove, Wavertree, just off the High Street, to cater for the growing Roman Catholic population of the locality. Messrs J. & B. Sinnott's design included a large steeple, but this never materialised.

The present-day Our Lady's presbytery, in Chesnut Grove, was originally built in 1867 by the Wavertree Baths Company. This short-lived private company operated the baths – the part of the building with the tall windows – as a commercial venture, and rented out the front of the building to the Wavertree Local Board of Health as public offices. For this reason, it is sometimes described as Wavertree's 'first town hall'. This photograph must have been taken very shortly after the building's completion. In 1870 the premises were purchased by the Roman Catholic authorities and converted to a church and school.

Above: This building on the corner of Grove Street and the High Street was Wavertree's first post office. It was demolished in the early 1870s and replaced by much larger shop premises. Rose Cottage – which remains to this day, with its long front garden and privet hedge – can just be seen at the right-hand edge of this photograph.

Left: One of the new shops built on the site of the old post office was John Broughton's boot works, 33 High Street. The gilt lettering on the shopfront advertised 'hunting, riding, walking, shooting and fishing boots and shoes, hand or machine sewn, made to measure on the shortest notice'.

Opposite below: In this early twentieth century view of the High Street, the garden wall of 17-21 is on the left and the Bank of Liverpool branch (now 'Chequers' pub) is on the right. As the old village properties were redeveloped, so the opportunity was taken to set back the building line and widen the roadway.

17 High Street Wavertree Residence of Mrs. Hemans. (Poetess) About 1830

Above: Liverpool-born Felicia Dorothea Hemans was one of the most famous poets of her day, but now she is remembered for just one line: 'The boy stood on the burning deck…' (from *Casabianca*). She only lived in Wavertree for three years; it is said that she left because she found the villagers too inquisitive! This Edwardian postcard shows a row of three houses – numbered 17, 19 and 21 High Street – all set back behind a high wall. Mrs Hemans' home was the one on the left. Nowadays the whole site is occupied by a used-car sales area.

Above: Until 1895 Wavertree formed part of Lancashire for policing purposes. From the 1840s onwards, converted houses in the High Street had been used as a base, but in 1879 the Lancashire County Constabulary erected this purpose-built police station at 65-69 High Street. The police moved out in 1967, and since 1992 the building has functioned as a pub/restaurant.

Opposite above: As recently as 1978, petrol cost less than 69p a gallon (equivalent to 15p per litre) at the service station at 199/201 Picton Road. Still standing, behind the pumps, were three of the houses known as Almond Terrace, which originally had front gardens extending to the main road.

Opposite below: These cottages at 47-51 High Street were demolished by Liverpool City Council, in the name of 'slum clearance', shortly after this photograph was taken in 1969. The Rose Vaults pub is visible on the right. Having lain derelict for ten years, the site of the cottages was landscaped in 1979 – at the suggestion of the Wavertree Society – and became the Rose Garden.

Above: This Edwardian view of the High Street shows Grove Terrace, before road widening led to the removal of the front gardens and trees. The house with the portico, on the right, is
24 High Street which served as a doctors' surgery for most of the twentieth century.

Left: Quilliam's stationery shop and newsagents was situated at 64 High Street. The building was demolished in the 1930s – along with the adjacent Anderton Square – to make way for the Wavertree Gardens flats (now 'Abbeygate Apartments').

Right: The Wavertree branch of Parr's Bank was at 70 High Street, on the corner of Prince Alfred Road opposite the Thatched House pub. Parr's Bank originated in Warrington but by 1900 it had set up numerous branches in the Merseyside area, later becoming part of the Westminster (now NatWest) Bank. The insignia on this photograph suggest that the building had been decorated in honour of the coronation of King George V, which took place in June 1911.

Below: Pye Street, viewed here from Prince Alfred Road on 25 July 1934, is a very narrow, elbow-shaped street running through to the High Street. All of the houses – including Bowers Buildings visible in the distance – were demolished in 1935 and the families who lived there were rehoused in the new Wavertree Gardens flats nearby. (Courtesy Liverpool Record Office, ref. 352 ENG/2/7077)

This unusual photograph, apparently taken from an upper floor of Hicks' warehouse, shows the new electric tram tracks being laid in the High Street in 1900. The buildings on the right are on the site of the present-day Job Centre. In the distance, the silhouette of the Picton Clock Tower can just be made out. Horse trams had arrived in Wavertree in 1881, linking the Coffee House terminus with the Liverpool Exchange business district.

Right: Greenwood's dairy, at 72 High Street opposite the Town Hall, *c.* 1887.

Below: Not all of the pre-Victorian buildings in Wavertree High Street have been demolished or altered out of all recognition. This row includes the only surviving Georgian bow-windowed shopfront in Liverpool. At the time the picture was taken, in 1978, the building concerned (No.102) was still a traditional cobbler's shop, and next door on the corner of Waterloo Street was a building contractors' workshop in what had once been the village police station.

Mrs Agnes White's shop, 108 High Street, c. 1915. The products advertised include 'Turf – the guaranteed cigarette', Hignetts Smoking Mixture, and Red Seal toffee. Next door, the Clock Tower pub offered Joseph Jones & Co.'s Knotty Ash Creaming Stout.

At 2 Church Road North, in the 1930s, was Carlin's tobacconists shop, surrounded by the large advertisement hoardings which were such a feature of this corner facing the Picton Clock Tower. Miss Winifred Carlin is seen here standing in the shop doorway. The times of Crosville bus services are displayed in a frame alongside, and productions at the Majestic Cinema and the Royal Court Theatre are conspicuously advertised.

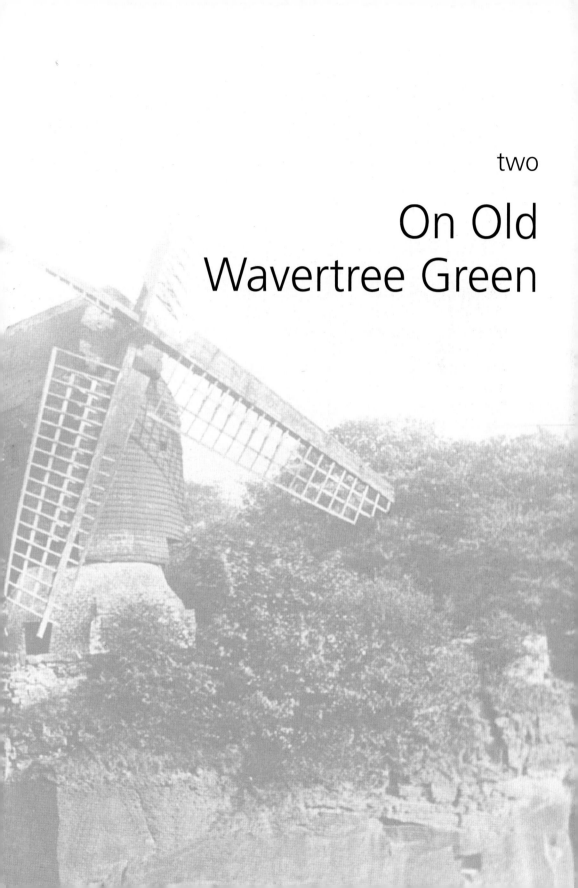

two

On Old
Wavertree Green

The large area of land once called Wavertree Green stretched from the village towards Childwall and eastwards from what is now Church Road. The Wavertree Enclosure Act of 1768 ordered this area to be divided up into fields, created a number of new roads, and made provision for safeguarding existing features such as the Ancient Well and the King's Mill.

Wavertree Lock-up and village green, Childwall Road, *c.* 1908. The triangular area of grass on which the lock-up stands is today the only piece of registered common land within the City of Liverpool. The sandstone lock-up was built in 1796, as a place to accommodate drunks and other petty criminals overnight. Its pointed roof with weathervane was added in 1869 by the architect and local historian James Picton, who lived nearby in Mill Lane. At that time it was threatened with demolition, as it was no longer required for its original purpose and was falling into disrepair. But Picton felt it was important to retain the building for its historic interest, and his scheme to 'beautify' it was accepted by the Wavertree Local Board of Health. The iron railings around the village green had been erected by the Local Board in 1864.

Right: The caption to this postcard, dated 1909, was 'The Old Prison-House, Wavertree'. A policeman poses for the photographer – but the building had not been needed for its original purpose since 1845 when a police station was opened in the High Street. Later uses of the lock-up included the isolation of cholera victims, the overnight accommodation of poor Irish people trekking inland to find work – and the storage of the village fire hose.

Below: An alternative name for the lock-up was the Round House – though it was octagonal! This boy was obviously on his way to Wavertree Lake, a favourite spot for fishing.

The roadway which links the Picton Clock Tower with Mill Lane is still called Lake Road, even though the lake itself was converted to a children's play area – the swing park – in 1929. This postcard shows the view across Lake Road from the village green.

Wavertree Lake, c. 1912. The row of ornamental trees separating the lake from Mill Lane was planted in the 1860s by the Wavertree Local Board of Health. It was lost in the 1920s when Mill Lane was widened following the filling in of the lake.

This photograph was taken in the summer of 1928. A year later, the lake had been filled in and the youngsters of Wavertree had to find other amusements. Ironically, child safety was one of the reasons given by the city council for removing the lake. Another reason was the need to widen Mill Lane to take electric trams.

Alongside the lake was the so-called Monks' Well – and a house of the same name which had been built on the site of the original Lake House. This house was later demolished to make way for new semi-detached housing, and in 1932 the developers presented the Monks' Well to Liverpool City Council to ensure its preservation.

Above: This 'artist's impression' of Wavertree's original public well shows the open archway above a stone basin containing the water. The site of the spring was on the lawn of Lake House, but in 1769 the well was moved so as to be closer to Mill Lane. The stone culverts – one bringing the water from the spring and another taking the overflow to the lake – gave rise to stories of 'secret passages' which have continued to the present day. The Latin inscription – traditionally translated as 'He who here does nought bestow, the Devil laughs at him below' – led to a belief that a monastery had once stood nearby, supported by donations from those drawing water.

Left: By 1864, when the Victoria Park estate was laid out with an access from Mill Lane, the well had fallen into disuse as Wavertree now had a piped water supply from Rivington. Later on, however, the sandstone cross was restored, and the well assumed the appearance we are familiar with today.

The Wavertree Enclosure Act provided for the creation of various new roads across the former 'commons and waste grounds' which it aimed to bring into more productive use. One of these roads became Lance Lane, forming the eastern boundary of the new and much-reduced Wavertree Green. No building was permitted on the western side of the road, but the eastern side – on the left of this picture – proved attractive to housing developers during the nineteenth century.

This was 15 Lance Lane, the home in the early twentieth century of Mabel Lowe. Mabel, who died in 2003 at the age of ninety-six, had many interesting memories of life in Wavertree. Next door at No.17 was the family joinery business – Matson's. The workshop at the rear caught fire when Mabel was five, and local gossips said it was because they had been working on a Sunday! The house itself survived until the 1960s.

One of the larger houses in Lance Lane was 'The Elms'. During the nineteenth century it had been home to a series of Liverpool merchants and other wealthy individuals, but in the early 1900s it was acquired by the Roman Catholic Order of Our Lady of the Cenacle and converted to a convent.

This was the rear view of 'The Elms', shortly after it became a convent.

About 1910 the old house was demolished and replaced by a purpose-built convent. The new building is seen here shortly after its completion, viewed from the field on the other side of Lance Lane. In 1991 a new and smaller convent was built on part of the site, the remainder now being occupied by the Tithebarn Close housing estate.

The Cenacle Convent must have been an idyllic place in the early years of the twentieth century. A lawn flanked by rhododendrons and roses, and surrounded by an 8ft-high wall, enabled peaceful and private meditation. Alongside, there was a large vegetable garden, an orchard, and an enclosure with hens, ducks and geese to keep the nuns supplied with food all year round.

A vestige of the old Wavertree Green survives as the Blue Coat School's playing field, bounded by Lance Lane, Woolton Road and Church Road North. Part of it is known as the 'Earle Field', it formerly having been the home of the Earle Football Club. This photograph shows the 1926/27 team, proudly displaying their trophies: the Lancashire Amateur Cup, the I Zingari Challenge Cup and the I Zingari Combination League Cup.

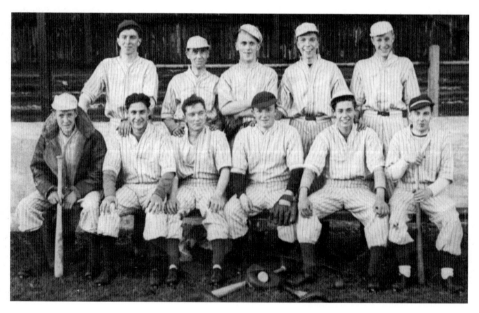

In the 1940s, the part of the playing field nearest to Church Road North was better known as a baseball ground, the 'Giants Field', after one of the resident teams. This photograph from 1946/47 shows the Liverpool Greys who also played there. Back row: H. Cohen, J. Hutton, N. Kynaston, K. Rayner, ? Wright. Front row: J. Wright, S. Moore, P. Hemmings, -?-, R. Lindforth, -?-.

The builders of the Abbey Cinema take a well-earned break, in front of the main entrance, in 1938. The cinema opened the following year. A court had ruled that the sole purpose of the ban on building on Wavertree Green was to safeguard the flow of wind to the sails of Wavertree Mill, and that, as the mill had been demolished over twenty years previously, it no longer had any relevance.

This was the Abbey Cinema – or Abbey Cinerama, as it had been called since 1964 – shortly after closure in the summer of 1979. The traditional hand-painted posters advertised the final film: *The Towering Inferno*. A few months later, the building was converted into a supermarket and bingo hall.

THE OLD MILL   WAVERTREE

Above: Wavertree Mill was not in Mill Lane! In fact it stood just off Woolton Road, to the east of Church Road. The sandstone hill was a useful source of building material, and the Enclosure Act reserved some land for quarrying alongside the mill. The extraction of stone proceeded rapidly during the nineteenth century from this quarry on the site of the present-day Tor View Road.

Delf and Mill, Wavertree.

Right: Even in its disused state, Wavertree Mill was a popular subject for artists and photographers. A great gale in 1895 had caused severe damage to the sails, though in fact the mill had ceased grinding corn in about 1890 when the final lease from the Marquess of Salisbury expired.

Below: The same scene in 1982. The mill had been demolished in 1916, and lock-up garages had later been built on the site at the junction of Beverley Road and Charles Berrington Road. But the mill cottages and the unmade trackway up from Woolton Road remained.

Opposite below: A 'delf' was the local dialect term for a stone quarry. The roof of Mill Cottage – the one-time miller's house – is visible in the centre of this picture, and on the right can just be seen the tower of Holy Trinity church. The quarry in the foreground is on the site of the present-day Mendip Road. Both quarries were filled in with household refuse during the early twentieth century, prior to houses being built in the 1930s.

Left: This postcard shows Wavertree Mill in an advanced state of dereliction, about 1910. It was a 'post' mill, the wooden superstructure being turned round on the brick base so that the sails could face the wind. A baulk of timber – seen here behind the stepladder – projected from the rear and was used to rotate the body of the mill.

Below: When planning permission was granted to build a pair of semi-detached houses on the site of the mill in 1986, a condition was imposed requiring an archaeological dig to be carried out. The brick foundations of the mill base and the stone blocks on which the struts supporting the main post had rested were exposed for the first time in many years. The archaeologists' conclusion was that, although there was documentary evidence dating Wavertree Mill back to the fifteenth century, when it was the property of the Crown and known as the King's Mill – the physical remains were no older than the eighteenth century.

three

The Slopes of Olive Mount

*O*live Mount is the name of the sandstone hill just north of Wavertree village, which attracted wealthy settlers in the nineteenth century seeking views over the surrounding countryside. Nearby, off Sandown Lane, is Victoria Park, a leafy residential estate which housed a good cross-section of Wavertree's middle classes during the Victorian era.

Olive Mount, Wavertree, Liverpool.

Above: This popular Edwardian postcard scene emphasised the still-agricultural feel of much of Wavertree. The cows are being driven up Mill Lane from the direction of the lake. The cottages on the right were demolished in the 1960s to make way for council housing. The junction with North Drive is in the foreground.

Left: The Georgian mansion called simply Olive Mount – viewed here in 1979 from one of the upper floors of the Olive Mount Heights tower flats – was built in the 1790s for James Swan, a wealthy Liverpool grocer and tea dealer. It is not clear whether the house gave its name to the hill or vice versa. The photograph shows the long-term effect of smoke pollution on the sandstone, the original pale cream colour of which has since been revealed by cleaning. In the grounds of the house, until 1991, was the Olive Mount Children's Hospital.

One of the 'villas' of the children's hospital – or the Wavertree Cottage Homes, as the institution was originally known – seen shortly before demolition in 1991. The idea of the cottage homes, when first built in 1901 by the Liverpool Select Vestry, was to enable orphans and other destitute children to live in family-type groups. This was a great improvement on the Victorian workhouse environment in which they had previously been accommodated.

Newstead in Mill Lane (now No.14 Old Mill Lane) was originally the home of Joseph Smith, a Victorian iron merchant. This photograph dates from about 1946, when it was the home of the Brandon family. Dr Rodney Brandon remembers: 'The stair banister and newel post were in polished mahogany and fitted with a heavy ornamental wrought-iron balustrade. Large black and white gravure prints of classic scenes from the Napoleonic wars hung in the stairwell in heavy gilt frames.'

Left: As an iron merchant, it is perhaps not surprising that Joseph Smith used ironwork extensively to decorate his house, its gates and balconies. The fire escape, though, is more modern – dating from the period when Newstead was converted to a Catholic children's home. This photograph was taken in 1979, shortly before the gates were removed and sold.

Below: Near the bottom of Mill Lane in the late nineteenth century stood Valencia House (its site commemorated by the present-day Valencia Road). It was the home of William M'George, fruit merchant, who presumably named the house after the source of his oranges.

Opposite below: Highfield and Selside, Olive Lane, *c.* 1905. In the late nineteenth century these two houses, built in the 1850s, were the home of a 'fringe manufacturer' and a window-blind manufacturer respectively.

Above: Sandown Hall, built for the Liverpool coal merchant Willis Earle in about 1810, occupied one of the finest sites close to the summit of Olive Mount. It enjoyed views to the west towards the growing town of Liverpool, the Mersey Estuary and the Welsh mountains beyond. Occupied for many years by the Russia merchant Hugh Hornby, and later by his daughters, it was acquired by Messrs Crawfords in the late 1920s and converted for use as a sports and social centre for their biscuit factory workers. This photograph was taken in 1969, when the field in front of the hall was used as a hockey pitch. In the 1970s parts of the grounds were sold off for housing development and in 1990, with the closure of the Binns Road biscuit works, the hall itself was sold. Plans for conversion to a nursing home came to nothing and in June 2000 – following two public inquiries – listed building consent for demolition was granted. The Halsnead Close housing estate now stands on the site.

A view of Sandown Hall taken from James Hoult's *West Derby, Old Swan and Wavertree* (1913). The three sisters – Helen Hornby, Mary Hornby and Mrs Matilda Madden – would have been living there at this time, their father having died in 1875 and their mother in 1881.

Sandown Hall in its derelict state, immediately prior to the second public inquiry (October 1998).

The upper section of Olive Lane, opposite Sandown Hall, *c.* 1905. The large semi–detached villas on the right were built in the 1850s.

In this view of Olive Grove from Mill Lane, the outbuildings of Sandown Hall and the spire of St Mary's church beyond are visible in the distance.

OLIVE MOUNT CUTTING,
NEAR LIVERPOOL.

Left: The Olive Mount Cutting was one of the engineering wonders of the Liverpool & Manchester Railway when it was opened in 1830. It was later widened and by 1900 was still regarded as a spectacular feature of the railways.

Below: Sandyknowe was the house built by James Picton in 1847 for himself and his family, on the very highest point of Olive Mount. He chose the site quite deliberately, modelled the house on Smailholm Tower in the Scottish border country, and named it after the adjacent farm where Sir Walter Scott grew up. Sir James Picton – knighted in 1881, largely owing to his promotion of public libraries as a Liverpool town councillor – died there in 1889. The red sandstone building, now converted to flats, is today much more easily visible from Mill Lane than when this photograph was taken in around 1906.

RAYMOND LODGE, LONG LANE, WAVERTREE.

Above: Raymond Lodge, *c.* 1905. Originally known as Olive Bank, this was another detached villa residence on the summit of Olive Mount. Today it is the home of the Liverpool Masonic Bowling Club.

Right: Long Lane – seen here in 1969, looking down from Olive Lane towards Sandown Lane – is one of the oldest roads in the Wavertree area. Many local residents still remember it in this unmade and unadopted state. On the right were the grounds of Sandown Hall and council-owned playing fields; on the left were the sports pitches and tennis courts of the Wavertree Recreation Company. This section of the road was made up in about 1974 when houses were built on some of the private recreation grounds.

Left: This only became an 'archive photograph' in September 2003 following the destruction of this historic pillar box by vandals, who had planted fireworks inside. Situated in Sandown Lane near the corner of Long Lane, it was one of only four surviving examples of the First National Standard box. The cast inscription on the base read: 'Cochrane Grove & Co., Woodside Works, Dudley 1865.'

Below: Sandown Lane, looking towards Sandown Park, *c.* 1906. On the left is the access road to Salisbury Terrace. On the right are the houses numbered 36–40, just before the cricket ground.

Opposite below: North Drive, Victoria Park, viewed from Sandown Lane in around 1923. Victoria Park was laid out as a private residential estate in the 1860s. The church (nowadays St Mary's Wavertree) was built for a Wesleyan Methodist congregation in 1872.

Above: The distant spire of the original St Mary's church can just be made out on this Edwardian postcard view of Sandown Lane. On the right, set back slightly from the road, is the row of houses known as Sandown Terrace, which had been built in about 1840. Early residents of the terrace included a butcher, a cotton broker, a customs officer, a nurseryman, a 'gentlewoman teacher', a clerk and a tobacco manufacturer.

Left: This was the original St Mary's church – not in North Drive, but in Sandown Park. Built in 1853, the church was a feature of this exclusive residential estate just west of Sandown Hall.

Below: Another Edwardian postcard view of St Mary's church. It was destroyed by bombing during the Second World War, and the congregation moved to the former Methodist building in Victoria Park.

Opposite below: Main entrance hall, Mabel Fletcher College, 1963. The reorganisation of further education provision in Liverpool in the 1990s led to its closure, and the buildings were demolished in 1997 to make way for the Bonchurch Drive housing estate.

St. Mary's Church, Sandown Park, Wavertree.

Above: Mabel Fletcher College was built in the early 1960s on the site of St Mary's church and the adjacent Sandown Grange. The college originated as the Wavertree Day Trade School for Girls, accommodated in the Technical Institute in Picton Road, offering full-time courses for girls preparing for careers in dressmaking and millinery. It later expanded considerably, and was renamed after Alderman Miss Mabel Fletcher.

An Edwardian view of South Drive, Victoria Park. The houses on the left – nowadays numbered 17 to 23 – were then named Heatherlea, Briar Holme, South View and Cloverley. In 1911 John Hicks the baker and corn dealer lived at Briar Holme, while next door at South View were Humphrey Nelson, barrister-at-law, and 'Madame Annie Nelson, vocalist'.

Rose Leigh, No.15 South Drive, *c.* 1906. According to *Gore's Directory of Liverpool*, it was the home of Thomas Adamson, draper, in 1903, but of William Earle, 'manager and receiver under Chancery', by 1911.

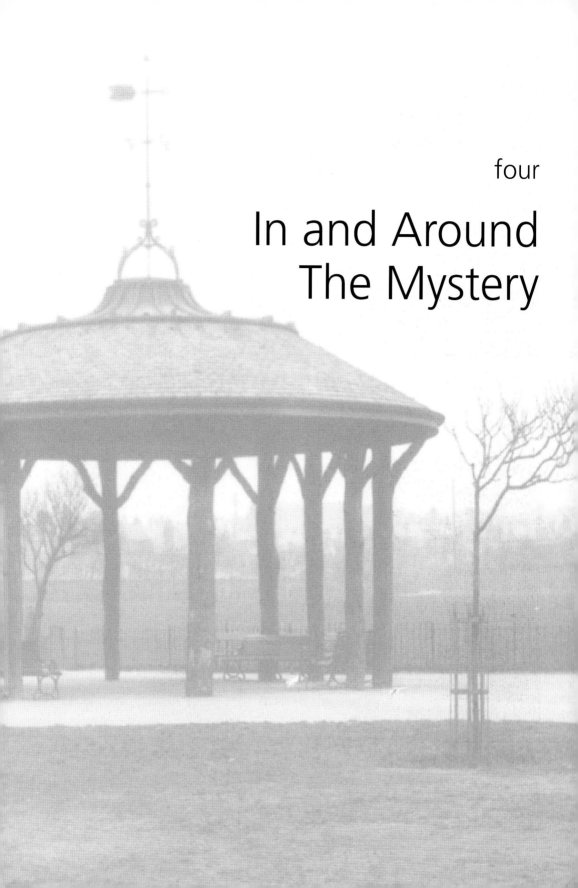

four

In and Around
The Mystery

The grounds of The Grange, a large house in Prince Alfred Road, were sold off in 1895. Instead of being covered in terraced housing, which was the normal fate of such estates in Liverpool at that time, the whole area was presented to the city by an anonymous benefactor, to be used for recreational purposes. The new park immediately acquired the nickname 'The Mystery'.

Above: The official name of the open space has always been Wavertree Playground. This postcard shows the Smithdown Road entrance in Grant Avenue, *c.* 1912.

Top: The anonymous donor intended the park as a place for sports and for children to run around, rather than for 'promenading'. This view, postmarked 1912, shows in the distance the School for the Blind (built in 1898) and, on the far right, the church of Holy Trinity. Unlike the earlier Liverpool parks, Wavertree Playground was not lavishly landscaped. Some of the trees which had decorated the grounds of The Grange were retained, though the ornamental lake was filled in.

Virtually all of the original park structures, such as this circular shelter, have since disappeared. But the nickname 'The Mystery' – or 'Mizzy' – has persisted. Nowadays the mystery to many local children is why their park has that name, rather than who the anonymous donor was!

The mysterious benefactor is, in fact, thought to have been Philip Holt the shipowner, who lived not far away and had become concerned at the lack of play space for youngsters as Liverpool expanded. As this postcard dated 1908 shows, the swings and see-saws were a very popular feature of the new park.

Playground, Wavertree.

This view from the early 1900s shows the hard-surfaced playground close to the Wellington Road entrance. In the background can be seen the roof of Rose Villa in Picton Road – nowadays the CAB building – and the swimming baths.

Wavertree Playground was not entirely situated within the old township of Wavertree. These stones – photographed in 1969 – were located alongside the railway embankment in the south-west corner of the park, and marked the boundary between the townships of Wavertree and Toxteth Park.

During the First World War, The Mystery was used for food production. The caption printed on this postcard was 'Bringing in the Sheaves. Wavertree Playground, Wartime 1917'.

The Mystery hosted a number of major events during the twentieth century, notably the annual Liverpool Show. In 1910 it was the venue for the Royal Agricultural Show. These were the temporary buildings at the Smithdown Road entrance.

Another postcard view of the buildings erected on The Mystery for the Royal Agricultural Show, 21-25 June 1910. The LNWR advertised easy access to the showground for passengers, cattle and goods.

Wavertree Gardens – the block of council flats in the High Street – always had a strong community spirit. In the late 1940s, after one of their frequent kickabouts in The Mystery, the lads formed a football team. The team players in the photograph (1949/50 season) are: Steve Riding, Bobby Glover, J. Munoz, Ken Hopkins, Reg Plunkett, John Robinson, Jackie Hornby, Terry (Spud) Murphy, David (Addy) Atherton, John Manning and Cyril Houghton. The background onlookers are: Billy Duncan, Jimmy Manning, Harold Citrine (coach), Eric Stanley, Pip Livingstone (assistant coach), Alf Plunkett, Robbie Burns, Ronnie Walsh, Johnny Glover, Billy Manning and Frankie Gleave.

Above: Hope Cottage, just inside the park gates at the end of Grange Terrace, survived until 1988. This photograph was taken in 1982 when it was used as a base for the grounds maintenance staff. Grange Court sheltered accommodation now occupies the site.

Right: The Grange itself was demolished at the time Wavertree Playground was laid out in 1895, but some of the other houses around the edge of the new park survived for a while – their rental income supporting the maintenance of the open space. This aerial view from the late 1920s shows Church Stile House, on the south side of Prince Alfred Road. Children are playing on the Blue Coat School's sports field just beyond.

Prince Alfred Road, originally Cow Lane, was renamed in 1866 in honour of Queen Victoria's second son, who had stayed at The Grange for two nights as the guest of Samuel Graves MP. This pre-1910 view shows how narrow the road once was. On the left is Barnhill Road, and on the right the grounds of Field House.

Another view along the southern part of Prince Alfred Road, this time from the opposite direction. Victoria Terrace is on the right. The curve of the road allowed the creation of front gardens, which were rare in Liverpool houses of this period.

An aerial view of the Blue Coat School in the late 1920s. In the bottom left-hand corner of the picture is Grant Avenue, laid out about 1910 when Field House was demolished. In the bottom right is the Liverpool Bowling Club's green on Church Road.

BLUE COAT SCHOOL, LIVERPOOL. Front showing Chapel.

The Blue Coat School – or Blue Coat Hospital, to give it its official title – was a charity school founded in Liverpool in 1708. By the end of the nineteenth century the trustees had decided to move out of the congested city centre into the countryside, and accordingly a site in Church Road, Wavertree was purchased. The new school opened in 1906. This early postcard view shows the main entrance – the clock tower not yet having been built – and the school chapel. The domed chapel had been presented by the shipowner Thomas Fenwick Harrison in memory of his wife Florence.

The Liverpool Blue Coat Hospital
Boys' Drill Squad

Many of the pupils at the Blue Coat School were orphans – the name 'hospital' merely signified that it was a residential institution – and great emphasis was placed on physical fitness as well as education. This postcard must date from after 1915, when the landmark clock tower was completed.

BLUE COAT SCHOOL, LIVERPOOL.
Girls' Play-Ground.

This card is postmarked 1913. The Blue Coat provided education and training for both boys and girls. Today – after a period as a boys-only school – it is once again co-educational, though boarders have not been accommodated since 1990.

The Blue Coat in the 1920s. Older residents of Wavertree remember being able to visit the school and watch the children eating from the balcony overlooking the dining hall. Former pupils particularly remember Christmas time, when giant puddings – some of them carried by four boys – were paraded around the dining hall, and eaten quickly in the hope of finding the silver threepenny bits!

The original purpose of the Blue Coat School, when founded in 1708 by seafarer Bryan Blundell and rector of Liverpool the Revd Robert Styth, was to teach poor children 'to read, write and cast accounts'. But the school also taught a variety of craft skills, and this tradition continued after the move to Wavertree. This card is postmarked 1930.

Above: The church of Holy Trinity was built in 1794 – a century before Wavertree Playground was created. Originally a chapel of ease to All Saints, Childwall, it became Wavertree's parish church in 1867. This view, from near the junction of Woolton Road and Church Road, shows the eastern end of the church in its pre-1911 form.

Below: In November 1910 the parishioners of Holy Trinity held a four-day 'Olde Wartre Bazaar' at Wavertree Town Hall, to raise funds for the new extension. Period costume was worn to recreate the atmosphere of 1794 when the church was first built.

Above: This photograph was taken shortly after 1911. Charles Reilly, Professor of Architecture at Liverpool University, was a friend of the Rector and had been commissioned to remodel the east end of the church in a Neo-Grec style. The elaborate stone 'lantern' at the other end was taken down for safety reasons in 1953.

Below: Holy Trinity School, in Prince Alfred Road, was nicknamed Cow Lane College – a reference to the original name of the road. Nowadays it is Wavertree Church of England School. Mabel Lowe witnessed the poverty of some of the pupils about the time of the First World War: 'Boys used to steal apples for breakfast from the boxes outside the greengrocers. The police used to go to Holy Trinity School regularly looking for culprits. My future brother-in-law felt very sorry for them, and always hoped they had already eaten the apples so they would not be hungry.'

Left: The gates of Wavertree Hall can still be seen in front of the Royal School for the Blind – but they are not original, and they are not gates either! This picture shows the view from inside the grounds during the nineteenth century. The story goes that, one night, the daughter of the house eloped through those gates with the coachman – as a result of which her distraught father ordered them to be locked for evermore. The present-day 'gates' are, in fact, ornamental railings installed in 1986 to recreate the appearance of the original, and to maintain the old tradition.

Below: This is a rare photograph of Wavertree Hall, which was demolished in 1898 to make way for the School for the Blind. In the late nineteenth century it was the home of John A. Smith, a 'general merchant', his family and four servants. This building, which stood facing what is now Church Road North, should not be confused with the 'other' Wavertree Hall – demolished in the mid-nineteenth century – on Wavertree Road, Edge Hill.

Above: In 1895, the township of Wavertree was absorbed into the City of Liverpool. Shortly afterwards, Liverpool Corporation built public baths and a library in Picton Road, backing onto The Mystery. The library was completed in 1903, and the baths in 1906. Both buildings were designed by the Corporation Surveyor, Thomas Shelmerdine.

Below: This view of the Wellington Road/Picton Road junction in 1978 remains largely unchanged today, except for the signage and the decoration of the buildings. The Wellington pub on the corner was originally an outlet for the Rose Brewery alongside, which for much of the twentieth century served as a bottling plant.

Above: Rose Villa, 242 Picton Road, is today the Wavertree Citizens Advice Bureau. From 1913 until 1939 it was the home of John Evans Bottrill, the manager of Heeley's bottling works next door. This photograph from about 1921 shows young Richard Bottrill visiting his grandmother.

Left: Richard Bottrill – seen here in the former greenhouse at the rear – lived in Rose Villa for several years, after his father Herbert took over as manager. He particularly remembered the old cannons, which were used as bollards to protect the gateposts of the yard next door. These were later moved closer to the house, when its front garden was converted to a car park.

At 102 Wellington Road was the shop and bakery of William Henry Crook. In the early 1900s local people could bring unbaked bread or hotpots and pay a small fee for them to be baked in the ovens. Mr Crook's two horses were stabled off Wimbledon Street.

Also in Wellington Road were the Wavertree Steam Mills of John Blyth. The building has long since disappeared – it was on the site of the present Bisley Street and Wimbledon Street – but this invoice from the 1860s shows that it incorporated an old windmill. John Blyth was a leading Congregationalist, associated with the chapel in Hunters Lane and, later on, its Wellington Road mission.

LNWR locomotive *Cornwall* at Wavertree Station, Wellington Road. The embankment which forms the western boundary of Wavertree Playground was created in 1863–64 as part of the Edge Hill & Garston Deviation. After the opening of the Runcorn Bridge in 1869, this provided a more direct route to London than the old Liverpool & Manchester Railway. The station closed to passengers and was demolished in 1959, though of course the railway line itself is still very much in use.

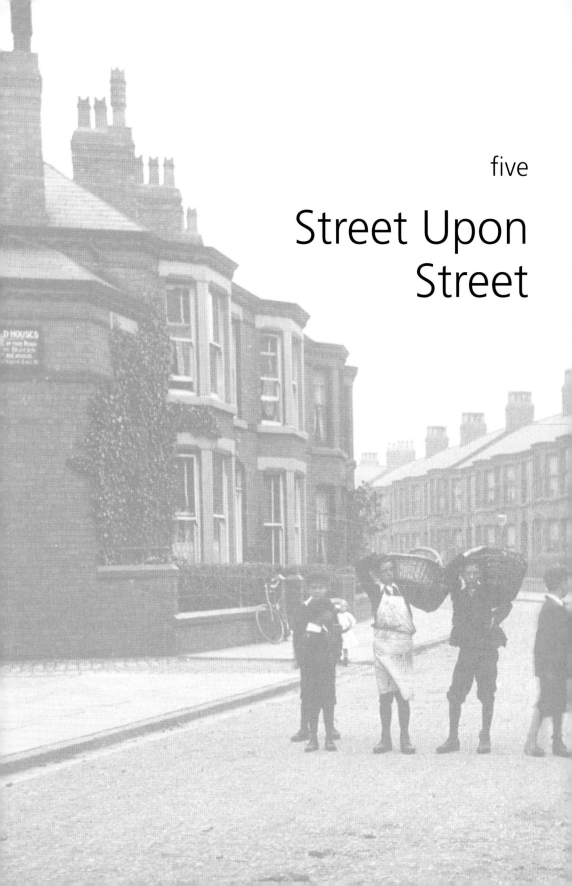

five

Street Upon Street

Between about 1870 and 1914, Liverpool's built-up area expanded rapidly as trams made it easy and relatively cheap for workers to travel in to the centre along all the major radial routes. In Wavertree, virtually the whole district between Picton Road and Smithdown Road became covered in solidly built terraced houses fronting onto parallel streets, the layout of the streets reflecting the old field patterns and the distance between the rows of houses being regulated only by the building bye-laws. Constructed by an army of Welsh builders, the area has remained a popular place to live for the past 100 years.

'In Penny Lane there is ...'. In fact most of the landmarks referred to in The Beatles' song – the shelter, the bank, the barber shop – are in Smithdown Place, Wavertree, which is in the bottom right-hand corner of this picture from the 1970s. Church Road runs up to the left, past the Prince Alfred Road bus depot, and on the other side of Church Road are the parallel terraced streets laid out by the builder Charles Berrington around 1910. The end of Penny Lane itself – part of which formed the ancient boundary between Wavertree and Toxteth Park – is just visible at the bottom of the photograph to the left of St Barnarbus' Church.

'Penny Lane' was the name of the tram and bus terminus – the reason for the shelter – at Smithdown Place. This photograph from around 1930 shows the 720-seater Presbyterian Church of Wales, which had been opened in 1927 – a visible reminder of the importance of the Welsh community in Liverpool.

Heathfield Road, viewed from the junction with Church Road, *c.* 1905. The building on the right was the coach house to Dudlow Cottage – a large house on the site of the present-day Welsh chapel.

WINDSOR HIGH SCHOOL, MAYFIELD, LIVERPOOL.

Above: In the late 1890s Liverpool was a pioneer in what we would today call recycling. Here in Smithdown Road were three municipal enterprises side by side: the tram sheds, an electricity generating station and – behind the wall on the left of this picture – a refuse destructor works. The domestic waste collected by the bin wagons was burnt here, producing electricity to power the trams, and leaving behind a large quantity of clinker which the City Engineer used for road building.

Opposite above: The house originally known as Mayfield – now an accountant's office – stands at the junction of Church Road with Heathfield Road. In 1827 it was the home of James Pownall, a Liverpool merchant. After the First World War it was the Windsor High School – an academy for young ladies.

Opposite below: As more and more houses were built, so there was a need for service providers, including dairymen, who often kept cows in shippons behind the terraces. This was the milk cart of James and Richard Atkinson, whose dairy was at 31 and 33 Heathfield Road on the corner of Coventry Road. The postcard is dated 1915.

Messrs Hargreaves had a number of branches around the city, initially specialising in fruit before diversifying into more general grocery. This postcard view of No.611 Smithdown Road is dated 1907.

The Brook House pub was technically not in Wavertree, as the boundary between Wavertree township and Toxteth Park broadly followed Garmoyle Road. But it is in the Liverpool 15 postal district, and it was designed by a Wavertree architect – John Elliot Reeve, who also designed Wavertree Town Hall. The name Brook House is a reference to the Upper Brook, which ran nearby and fed the river Jordan, entering the Mersey at Otterspool.

Lidderdale Road, viewed from the Smithdown Road end, *c.* 1905.

Ferndale Road, like Lidderdale Road, runs from Smithdown Road to Garmoyle Road and beyond. In the early 1900s the householders here included an engineer, a bottle merchant, a wine merchant, a manager, a mariner, a schoolmaster and a tailor.

No.431 Smithdown Road was a confectioner's shop, the sunblind of which advertised 'Cyclists catered for'. Appropriately enough, a bike is parked outside. Next door at No.429, W.E. Jackson was a cabinet maker and house furnisher. The turning on the right is Ferndale Road.

Posing for the camera at the Smithdown Road end of Brookdale Road, in the summer of 1906. The large building on the left was a branch of the Liverpool Co-operative Society.

This view of Smithdown Road probably dates from the 1930s. On the right is the junction with Brookdale Road.

The houses in Avondale Road are to this day characterised by decorative terracotta pediments above the single-storey bay windows. In this postcard view dated 1905, a horse-drawn bread van makes its way along the street.

The Gregson Memorial Institute and Museum in Garmoyle Road was opened in 1897. It was erected by Miss Isabella Gregson 'for scientific recreation' in memory of her father, mother, brother and sister, all of whom had died between 1876 and 1884. The museum was relatively short-lived, its collections being transferred to the city museum and the university from 1933, before the sale of the institute building to Liverpool Corporation in 1936. It is now a Scout and Guide hall.

This view of Smithdown Road, dated 1912, features a large 'millinery establishment' at No.397, on the corner of Avondale Road. In the distance is the tower of St Columba's English Presbyterian church, just beyond the junction with Ullet Road.

Kenmare Road, looking from Smithdown Road towards Garmoyle Road, *c.* 1905. *Gore's Directory of Liverpool* indicates the occupiers of the houses on the right as including a postal clerk, a tailor, a GPO inspector and a builder.

Marie (*née* Trotter) – seen here in the driving seat of her husband's car in 1926 – was one of seven daughters of a ship-repair manager. The family ran a confectioner's shop here at 371 Smithdown Road, but Marie and her husband emigrated to Trinidad shortly after this picture was taken.

Between Blantyre Road and Barrington Road stands this distinctive block of shops, seen here in around 1913. On the left of the photograph, at 349 Smithdown Road, is Atherton Bros: 'Plants and flowers a speciality'. The cart on the right belongs to John Mason, the well-known Wavertree removal contractors.

Gainsborough Road, c. 1907. The picture was taken from Garmoyle Road. In the distance is the railway bridge over Wellington Road, adjacent to Wavertree Station.

This Edwardian postcard view of Smithdown Road is dated 1909. It includes Woodhall & Son's bakery at No.337, on the corner of Gainsborough Road. On the right can be seen the entrance to the Quaker burial ground (which, like this stretch of Smithdown Road itself, was in Toxteth Park rather than Wavertree township).

Woodcroft Road, *c.* 1907. The street name is a reminder of the house which once stood nearby. The grocery/tobacconist's shop on the left (at the rear of 271 Smithdown Road) no longer exists.

The curved alignment at the south end of Portman Road was necessitated by the existence of older houses in Smithdown Road. The date of the postcard is 1908. The wooden sign on the left – on the side wall of No.1 – advertises 'Freehold houses for sale in this road, singly or in blocks'.

Egerton Road, viewed from the Lawrence Road end, in the early 1900s. In 1911 the householders included a printer, a mason, a joiner, a commercial traveller and an articled clerk.

This postcard of Langton Road, viewed from the Smithdown Road end, bears the handwritten date 1906. The horse-drawn delivery van in the distance belongs to MacSymons Stores – a Liverpool-based firm selling groceries and household products, which had branches both within and outside the city. On the left are the premises of Thomas Goss, cowkeeper.

This was Lawrence Road in the early 1900s. On the far left is Mrs Lilian Dunn's chandlery, with Miss Etty McAusland's fancy goods shop next door at No.39. The side turning a little further along is Cretan Road. Lawrence Road was originally intended as a major route into and out of Liverpool. In 1857 it was referred to in the Local Board's minutes as 'Childwall Road' – the intention at that time being to continue it across what later became Wavertree Playground and link into Fir Lane. The name Lawrence Road – after Henry Lawrence, a local landowner – was adopted in 1866.

Left: St Bridget's church was built on the corner of Lawrence Road and Bagot Street between 1868 and 1872 – in advance of many of the surrounding houses. Its architect was Edward Heffer, and its brick tower has always been a landmark in the midst of this vast area of terraced streets. Sir Nikolaus Pevsner, in his *Buildings of England: South Lancashire*, described the church as 'a real basilica'.

Below: 'Liverpool Elementary Schools Gala, September 1897. St Bridget's School, Wavertree, Swimming Squadron'. The handwritten caption on this photograph names the boys as H. Crook, J.W. Bird, W.J. Farquhar and E.J. Fox. Harold Crook was the son of the baker in Wellington Road. His daughter recalls that one of the boys went on to work as a submarine miner at the mouth of the Mersey during the First World War.

The historic boundaries of the townships surrounding Liverpool became almost irrelevant after 1895, when the city expanded to include Wavertree, Walton and West Derby. But, as recently as 1969, these metal pillars could still be seen marking the western edge of the township of Wavertree, cutting across Wavertree Park close to Botanic Road. The cylindrical marker had been erected by Wavertree, and the more elaborate one by the West Derby authorities.

Like many of Liverpool's Victorian 'locals', the Leigh Arms in Picton Road is no longer in use as a pub. (This picture was taken in 1969.) Built in 1859, it was named after the landowner John Shaw Leigh.

Above: Posing for the photographer on busy Picton Road would not be quite as safe nowadays! This group are standing on the corner of Salisbury Road – its name a reminder that the Marquess of Salisbury was the leading landowner here, as well as being Lord of the Manor of Wavertree – in about 1907. Behind them is Mrs Margaret Lloyd's drapers shop at 50 Picton Road.

Left: James Lumley's shop was at 68 Picton Road – between Kempton Road and Alderson Road. In addition to the 'high-class confectionery', a notice on the front door offers meat pies for sale. The postcard is dated 1907.

Right: This was Edward Radforth's butchers shop at 106 Picton Road – between Ashfield and Kempton Road. The handwritten caption on the original postcard reads: 'Uncle Ted Radforth and his Man'.

Below: Ashfield, on the south side of Picton Road (or Wavertree Road, as it was known until 1883) was in existence as a street, but not yet named, on the Ordnance Survey map published in 1851. This was long before the surrounding area was developed. Some of the original Victorian villas have been lost over the years – including this pair of semi-detached houses, Nos 35/37 Ashfield, photographed in 1979. The tower of St Thomas's church is in the distance.

This terrace of houses in Ash Grove has long since disappeared – the victim of a powerful bomb which fell here during the Second World War. The picture shows the east side of the street, looking south from Picton Road, *c.* 1905. The householders at that time included a large number of engine drivers and other railway employees.

Wavertree Vale, *c.* 1905. Now redeveloped as Picton Crescent and Ash Vale, this was another enclave of housing on the south side of Picton Road which already existed by 1858. The Belle Vue pub, on the left, advertises Staffordshire Ales. The name 'Belle Vue' was a reference to a house which formerly stood on the opposite side of Picton Road, reached by means of a long driveway. The house itself must have been demolished at about the time the pub was built, to make way for the new Edge Hill-Garston railway line. The railway – which had a goods station near here – later provided work for many of the residents of Wavertree Vale and surrounding areas.

This view of Macdonald Street, looking towards Picton Road, dates from about 1905. On the right can just be seen the grocery shop on the corner of Broadwood Street. Among the other occupiers of the houses in this picture were a painter, a baker and a gardener.

As Liverpool expanded, there must have been plenty of work for removal contractors in places such as Wavertree. Fletcher & Son, whose yard was at 172 Picton Road, just alongside the railway bridge, advertised their services as 'removers and storers to families removing or warehousing'.

Above: Jackson's sweetshop, 204 Picton Road, *c.* 1903. Signs in the window advertise ice cream, pies and sandwiches for sale. Reflected in the glass is the building on the corner of Hey Green Road opposite. Standing in the doorway are John Edward Jackson – son of the owner, William Walker Jackson – and his wife Laura.

Opposite above: This was 'Group 6' at Hey Green Council School in about 1915. Thomas Owen – the uncle of the owner of this photograph – was in the second row of desks from the left, and three rows back.

Opposite below: This view of Taunton Street, looking north from Picton Road in the early 1900s, shows the site prepared for the construction of Hey Green Council School. About ninety years later the school was demolished, having been replaced by a brand-new building – but the houses remain.

The last remaining 'gap' between Wavertree village and the main built-up area of Liverpool was sealed in about 1910, when the grounds of Westdale House – opposite the former Rose Brewery in Picton Road – were sold off to developers and became covered in houses and shops. The sunblinds on the left of this picture advertise some of the early traders: W. Partington the tobacconist at No.129, Hamilton & McCulloch the grocers at 131, and John Moyles the fishmonger at 133. A branch of Hargreaves the fruiterers can be seen on the far corner of Westdale Road.

Westdale Road, looking up towards Northdale Road, *c.* 1913. The relatively unusual round-bayed houses were the work of Messrs Jones & Hughes, two men who came originally from Anglesey. This particular Jones was, apparently, nicknamed 'Drinkwater' owing to his refusal to give bricklayers the customary 'price of a pint' on completing the first house in a block!

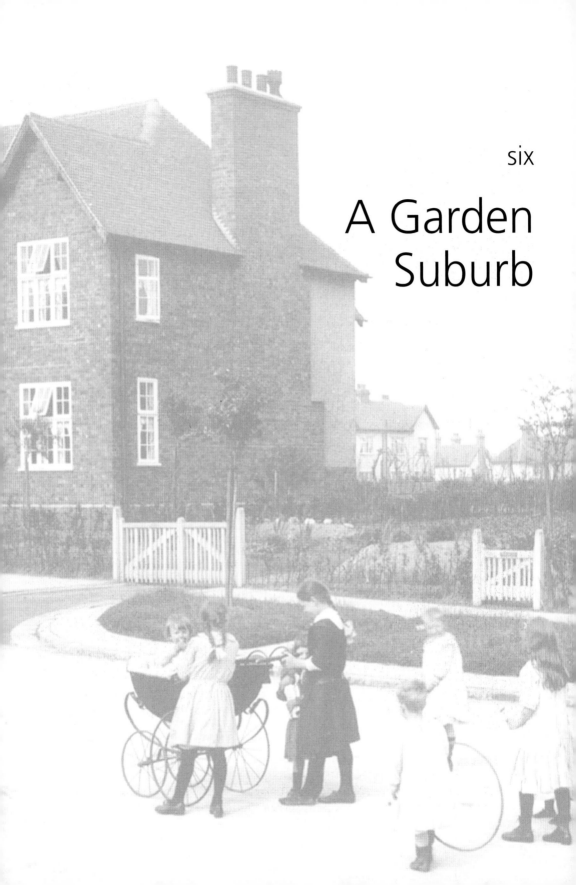

six

A Garden Suburb

Wavertree was one of the areas chosen for an experiment in housing reform in the years just prior to the First World War. The Liverpool Garden Suburb, alongside the newly constructed Queens Drive ring road, was one of about fifteen developments in various parts of England and Wales sponsored by Co-partnership Tenants Ltd of London. In addition to houses with gardens – a rarity in Liverpool at that time – the plans included recreational and social facilities, all designed to create a sense of community. The outbreak of war, however, meant that only 360 out of the planned 1,800 houses were ever built.

Above: One of the early Wavertree Garden Suburb residents commented, in 1914, 'we were the pioneers'. Some people thought it slightly eccentric that anyone should want to live in such a remote place, which involved a ten-minute trek along Thingwall Road from the tram terminus at the Picton Clock Tower. This early postcard photograph shows the new suburb viewed across the fields from Childwall Road.

Top: This view of Nook Rise dates from 1911, immediately after the houses there were completed. In the distance, the houses in Southway (then called North Way) are still under construction. The roadside trees were a great feature of the Garden Suburb, and in Nook Rise each of the new trees was planted by a child living nearby.

The foundation stone of the first house in Wavertree Garden Suburb was laid by the Marchioness of Salisbury on 20 July 1910. The house concerned was the present No.13 Wavertree Nook Road, which is in the centre of this picture.

This picture was published in Volume Two of the *Town Planning Review*, which took a keen interest in the progress of the new estate. It shows Wavertree nook Road, at its junction with Nook Rise, in the summer of 1911. While all the houses in Wavertree Garden Suburb were initially rented, the tenants were encouraged to buy shares in the company which owned the estate. This was the principle of 'co-partnership' which, it was hoped, would spread the benefits of property ownership more widely – as well as keeping maintenance costs down.

Thingwall Road, like Wavertree Nook Road, was a pre-existing highway at the time the Garden Suburb was created. The houses on Thingwall Road were among the largest to be built, some of them having six bedrooms whereas some of those in Nook Rise had only two. The idea was to create a mixed community, within which the tenants could move around as their families grew.

The houses in Thingwall Road were still under construction when this social gathering of Garden Suburb residents took place in 1911. Perhaps this is one of the 'al fresco concerts' referred to in an early issue of the *Town Planning Review*.

An early Garden Suburb sports day, held on the field behind Nook Rise, Wavertree Nook Road and Thingwall Road.

By 1912 a tennis court and bowling green had been laid out for the benefit of the tenants. In the background are the houses in Nook Rise.

Above: In 1912 two former farm cottages were knocked together to form an Institute – or 'temporary clubhouse', as it was referred to at the time. The groups meeting there in 1913 included the Ambulance Class, the Choral Society, the Horticultural Society, the Magazine and Book Club, the Thingwall Players and the Women's Social Guild. The intention was to erect a purpose-built Wavertree Garden Suburb Institute on Queens Drive, but that never happened. The 'temporary' premises are still in use, though by the time this picture was taken in 1979 the 'Saturday evening meetings of the Discussion Society' had given way to bingo!

Opposite above: In North Way – viewed here from Thingwall Road – an avenue of may trees was planted on the new grass verges. These flowering hawthorns have remained a valued feature of the area ever since.

Opposite below: The gate at the far end of North Way marked the boundary of the land which Liverpool Garden Suburb Tenants Ltd had leased from Lord Salisbury. After the First World War, Liverpool Corporation built an estate of council houses on the other side of the boundary, and extended North Way to serve the new development. As a result, the tenants of the Garden Suburb houses petitioned for their addresses to be changed – and the original section of the road was renamed 'Southway'.

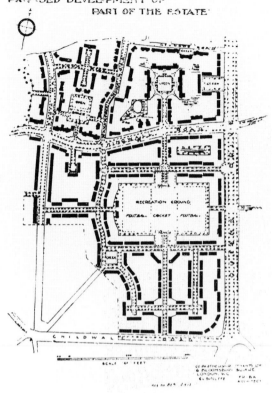

LIVERPOOL GARDEN SUBURB TENANTS LTD.
PROPOSED DEVELOPMENT OF
PART OF THE ESTATE

Left: The pattern of streets and houses in the Garden Suburb was very different from the Liverpool norm. This plan, published in 1912, showed the proposed layout to the west of Queens Drive – including parts of the estate which, in the event, were never built.

Below: The developers of the Garden Suburb had to make a positive effort to tempt new residents to move there. Promotional brochures were produced, one of which in 1914 included this photograph: 'A corner of North Way, showing the way in which pleasant vistas are obtained at every point'. The view referred to is between the houses now numbered 34 and 35 Southway.

The first tenants of 'Cotehill' – No.13 North Way – pose for the camera: Ernest, Mary, Palmer and (seated) their sister Gertrude Martin. In 1910 young Ernie happened to get a job as a bricklayer on the Garden Suburb. He was so impressed by the scheme that he went home to tell his father, who was also a bricklayer by trade. The result was that in 1911 the whole family moved from Milroy Street, Edge Hill, into one of the new houses. Tom Martin, the father, soon became a leading light in the social life of the suburb, while daughter Mary – a student teacher – organised the dancing at the suburb's summer festivals and was secretary of the Women's Social Guild.

The clay-tiled roofs, roughcast walls and small-paned casement windows of the Garden Suburb were derived from traditional English cottage architecture, and were quite unlike the red-brick, slate-roofed terraces which had been the norm in Liverpool for over fifty years. This was Nook Rise, viewed from North Way, in about 1914.

The twin cul-de-sacs of Nook Rise were another innovation of the Garden Suburb's designer, Raymond Unwin – who went on to become the government's chief adviser on town planning matters. The idea was to save money on road construction – but also to encourage a sense of community. This photograph must date from 1911, when work on the recreation ground and the houses in Thingwall Road beyond was still in progress.

These houses – 'Carreg Wen' and 'Arlington' on the east side of Wavertree Nook Road (nowadays numbered 46 and 44 respectively) – were part of the second phase of the Garden Suburb, which commenced in 1912.

The lack of shops was one of the few complaints of the 'pioneer' settlers. It was left to the Toxteth Co-operative Provident Society to build a store in Wavertree Nook Road – just outside the official boundary of the Garden Suburb – in 1914, and other small shops eventually followed. This photograph dates from the late 1920s.

When first published in 1914, the caption to this photograph read: 'Heywood Green. Houses from 8s per week'. This eight shillings was comparable to the weekly rent being charged by private landlords at that time, for houses which did not have the benefit of a garden.

The designer of the second phase of the Garden Suburb was an architect called George Lister Sutcliffe, who had written textbooks on house design and sanitation. Apart from the individual gardens front and back, he liked to provide communal 'greens' such as this one in Fieldway, and groups of allotments tucked away behind the houses.

One of the reasons why this corner of Wavertree was chosen as the site of the Liverpool Garden Suburb was the existence of the new 'circumferential boulevard' – Queens Drive, laid out by Liverpool's City Engineer John Brodie. The stretch between the Rocket bridge and what was to become the Fiveways junction was originally Priory Road – the historic boundary between Wavertree and Childwall – but Brodie converted it to a dual carriageway in 1910. This was the view, looking south towards Thingwall Road, in about 1912.

This photograph shows the section between Heywood Road and the Rocket in the late 1920s – when traffic volumes were still very low!

Left: On 4 July 1914, Earl Grey – a great supporter of the co-partnership housing movement – came to Liverpool to lay the foundation stone of the new Garden Suburb Institute on the west side of Queens Drive, about 200 yards south of Thingwall Road. The architect, G.L. Sutcliffe, explained that 'the large central hall will be able to seat close upon 500 people, and the other parts of the building include three billiard-rooms (one of which will probably be reserved for ladies), reading, games, dressing and refreshment rooms'.

Below: The Countess Grey laid another foundation stone alongside, and several speeches were made extolling the virtues of Garden Suburbs. Unfortunately, though, the First World War broke out exactly one month later – and the new institute got no further than these first two stones.

LADY GREY LAYS STONE
GARDEN SUBURB.

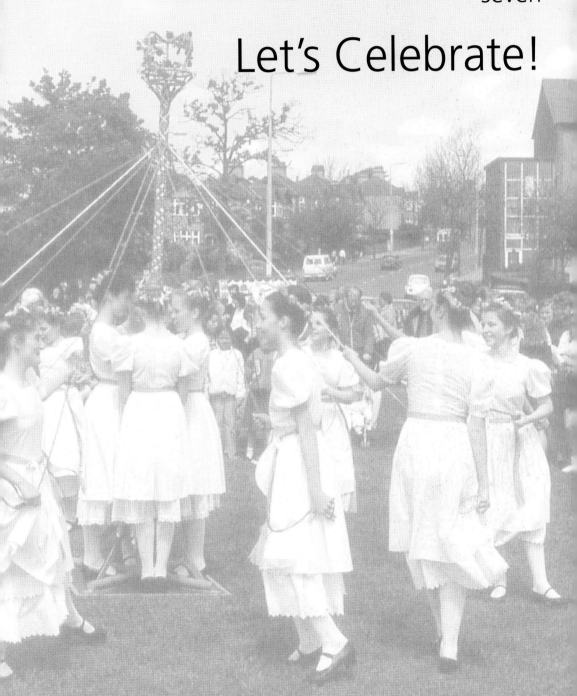

seven

Let's Celebrate!

*V*illage traditions such as maypole dancing and the crowning of the Rose Queen have long been popular subjects for the photographer. In Wavertree, such traditions were consciously 'revived' during the twentieth century, especially within the Garden Suburb which set out to create a strong community spirit among its residents. Wavertree has also taken part in citywide and national celebrations over the years, many of which have been caught on camera.

Above: Empire Day was celebrated in Liverpool schools, as elsewhere, right through until the 1950s. It took place each year on 24 May – Queen Victoria's birthday. This was the Northway Council School line-up in 1936, when pupils were allowed to dress in whatever costume they liked!

Top: In June 1866 Queen Victoria's son Prince Alfred, Duke of Edinburgh, visited Liverpool. Among other things he laid the foundation stone of the Children's Infirmary in Myrtle Street and opened a new dock entrance on the other side of the river Mersey. He stayed as the guest of Samuel Graves MP at The Grange, Cow Lane – which was renamed 'Prince Alfred Road' in his honour – and the villagers turned out in force to welcome him.

Lawrence Road School took its celebrations very seriously – and made sure they were properly recorded. This was Empire Day in 1914 – just before the outbreak of war.

Another 'group' photograph from Lawrence Road School, this time May Day in 1908, complete with maypole in the playground. The school itself has now been redeveloped, but the houses in Tabley Road behind survive.

'Better Education' and 'Peace' were the slogans on this May Day float, pictured outside the Garden Suburb home of Councillor Mrs Hamilton in the late 1920s. Mrs Hamilton – a Labour member of Liverpool City Council – lived at 107 Thingwall Road, and encouraged local children to take part in the city's annual parade. The children were impressed by the fact that she went to Russia on holiday – and that she could get them tickets for the Lord Mayor's party!

Wavertree Garden Suburb's first summer festival took place in June 1912. Miss Mary ('Molly') Martin paraded her dance troupe on the temporary stage by the tennis court, backing on to Wavertree Nook Road.

By the summer of 1913 a new and very appropriate venue was available for the Garden Suburb's festival: Fieldway Green.

The morris dancers make their way towards Fieldway Green. The balcony attached to 56 Fieldway was purpose-designed for observing the festivities. On 4 July 1914 an even more elaborate celebration took place here, when a pageant was held following the laying of the foundation stones for the new Garden Suburb Institute. The theme was 'Scenes of Village Life, 1100-1914, in Five Episodes' which culminated in a comparison between an ordinary suburb and a Garden Suburb. As the *Liverpool Daily Post* commented afterwards: 'For the latter the only scene needed was Fieldway Square itself, which was looking its prettiest in the bright sunlight'.

Above: The architect G.L. Sutcliffe had envisaged Fieldway Green as the site of new tennis courts, but in the event it was left as an informal play area and the venue for summer festivals such as this.

Below: The first scene in the 1914 pageant was a re-creation of Saxon and Norman village life – the backdrop being a Norman castle entrance.

Right: A memorable series of Floral Queen Festivals took place in the Garden Suburb during the 1930s. The venue was no longer Fieldway Green, but the LOGOS (now Scottish Power/Manweb) sports ground on Thingwall Road.

Below: Local Girl Guides and Boy Scouts provide a guard of honour for Floral Queen Nora Lawson at the 1929 festival. In the background are the houses in Southway.

LIVERPOOL GARDEN SUBURB FLORAL QUEEN FESTIVAL

ON SATURDAY, JULY 1ST, 1933

CROWNING OF THE FLORAL QUEEN SPORTS - MAYPOLE & MORRIS DANCES

PROGRAMMES 6 D. EACH

Above: The participants in the 1929 Garden Suburb Festival pose for the camera. A later programme explained the procedure for selecting the Floral Queen: 'Every child in the Suburb between the ages of five and fifteen is invited to a meeting at the institute. Then every child is given a ballot paper upon which he or she shall write the name of his or her choice. The children are given a free hand in the matter, and the only conditions which they themselves have imposed are that the Queen must reside in the Suburb, that she must have been a maid-of-honour or a flower girl in a previous year, and must not have been crowned in the Suburb before.'

Opposite above: The Institute in Thingwall Road remained a focal point of Garden Suburb life. Floral Queen Freda Smith is seen here leaving the building in 1930.

Opposite below: Freda Smith proudly wears her Dowager Queen's crown in June 1931, accompanied by her (mostly!) happy entourage of train-bearers and fairies.

Pauline Littlewood, the Floral Queen in 1931, is here accompanied by Gary Griffith (crown-bearer), Donald Moulds (mace), Peter Batten (sceptre), Ian Henry and Kenneth Davies (train-bearers).

Joan Allen was Floral Queen in 1932 – the ceremony having been performed by the Lady Mayoress, Mrs Cross.

A scene in the garden of 32 Wavertree Nook Road prior to the 1933 festival. Floral Queen Marie Henry poses with 'bridegroom' Trefor Griffith, herald Gary Griffith, and train-bearers Stanley Lewis and Ian Henry. As in previous years, the ceremony was arranged and produced by Trefor and Gary's parents, Mr & Mrs Meirion-Griffith.

Beefeaters on parade at the Garden Suburb Festival, 1938. The tall staff-bearer was Gordon Martin who, having joined the RAF, was tragically killed in December 1939.

The formal line-up at the 1938 Garden Suburb Festival. Floral Queen Zena Holland had been crowned by local radio personality 'Auntie Muriel' (Mrs Fayer-Taylor).

Zena Holland and her retinue, walking past the Cottage Homes at the 1938 festival.

In 1930, the centenary of the opening of the Liverpool & Manchester Railway was celebrated with a pageant on The Mystery.

The theme of the pageant was 'transport through the ages' – from the camel and the elephant to the stagecoach and the Rocket locomotive.

Celebrating the Queen's Silver Jubilee in 1977 at Northway Primary School.

A Silver Jubilee street party in Granard Road, 1977, organised by Mary and Mel Price.

A street party in Wavertree Nook Road, 1945. The residents of the southern section of Wavertree Nook Road were celebrating VE Day. Standing at the back are Harry Jennion, Pat Lowthian, Barbara Fairclough and Gerard Pattison.

The maypole returns to Wavertree in 1987. The Wavertree Society decided to celebrate its tenth birthday by reviving the old 'Wavertree Wakes Fayre' on the swing park in Mill Lane – just across the road from the village green. The girls of the Elliott-Clarke School provided some appropriate entertainment. The event was inspired by a 100-year-old newspaper article, which reported the drunken antics of the villagers and visitors to the Wavertree Wakes at that time. So, in the interests of public safety, alcoholic drink was strictly 'off limits' in 1987!

Other local titles published by Tempus

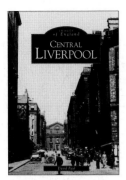

Central Liverpool

DAVID PAUL

This collection of 200 archive photographs, many drawn from the archive held by Liverpool Central Library, not only depicts the cosmopolitan face of Liverpool but also illustrates the nature and character of changes in the city over the last century. This isn't just a story based around grand buildings, it's about the ordinary people of the city who have made Liverpool great.

7524 0640 X

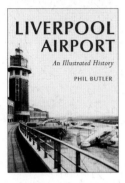

Liverpool Airport

PHIL BUTLER

From its official opening in 1933 to recent developments, this detailed history recounts the story of one of the North West's major airports. The airport played an extensive role during the Second World War: an RAF station was established at Speke and was also the base for several 'shadow' factories producing Blenheims, Stirlings and Halifaxes. The airport plans to welcome at least 3 million passengers each year.

7524 3168 4

Liverpool Docks

MICHAEL STAMMERS

The story of Liverpool is, in many ways, the story of its docks. With contemporary illustrations of people, ships, buildings and machinery, Michael Stammers chronicles not just the rise and fall of Mersey shipping but also the way the docks have bounced back. Redevelopment, restoration and new modes of commerce have put Liverpool's docks back in the black, albiet looking very different to the port of sixty years ago.

7524 1712 6

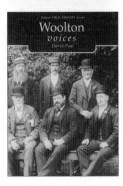

Woolton Voices

DAVID PAUL

This book brings together the memories of people who have lived and grown up in the village of Much Woolton during the twentieth century. The contributors include shopkeepers, teachers, labourers and many others, and the anecdotes give a flavour of the rich and diverse history of Woolton. The stories are complemented by over 100 photographs drawn from the personal collections of the storytellers.

7524 2617 6

If you are interested in purchasing other books published by Tempus, or in case you have difficulty finding any Tempus books in your local bookshop, you can also place orders directly through our website

www.tempus-publishing.com